The

Energy Alchemy

A Guide to Chakra Balancing

for the

Curious Creatrix

Connect to your

Purpose, Potential, Power & Passion

ISBN: 979 8 7607 8081 2

Contents

To the amazing women in my life who have taught and continue to teach me about courage, love, strength, humility, laughter, joy and connection.

Some of you I have known for many years and some only a short while, but you have all helped to shape who I am today, and for that, I thank you.

When we ladies come to circle, stand tall shoulder to shoulder, dust each other down, straighten each other's crowns, look each other in the eye and say *you've got this*, then the most amazing energy is created. Energy that transcends all space and time so that no matter where in the world you now live, no matter how long it's been since I saw you last, know that I hold a little piece of each and every one of you in my heart.

There are too many of you to name individually, but you'll know who you are.

To my wonderful family, none of this would have been possible without all of your love and support.

Forever grateful, I love you all deeply.

Hello & Welcome

If you are reading this now, it means divine timing has presented this book to your awareness for a reason.

An awakening has begun, an up-level of your energy to a new vibration, where it's time to weave some energy alchemy into your life.

It means that you've felt it.

That shift in your conscious mind as you're beginning to ask questions and are curious to explore what more there is to be offered in this world.

Questions such as:

> *What is my purpose here on Earth?*
> *What is my potential and how do I access it?*
> *How do I step into my personal power?*
> *What am I truly passionate about?*

> *Who am I, and what did I come here to do, be and have?*

I hear those questions and it means that you're ready.

> Ready to step out of the shadows and into the light.
> Ready to live unapologetically as the Creatrix of your own life.
> Ready to be the wild woman you came here to be: curious, strong, empowered, wise and free.
> Ready to look after all those you love and still have time for yourself.
> Ready to invest in yourself as an energetic being, to make those long-awaited changes.

As you read through this book you will have the opportunity to find many of the answers you seek.

As you begin to pay attention to your energy you will activate the process of release.

The more stagnant energy you release, the more space you will create.

The more space you create, the more you will feel into and trust your intuition.

The more you feel into and trust your intuition, the clearer the answers will become for you.

Here you will:

> ➤ Learn what chakras are, where they reside and how to balance them. You can then transmute all of the negative energy that you may currently be holding there.

> ➤ Read about the 4 types of energy that you have access to every day, and the 7 cups you fill with them.

> ➤ Learn which crystals can support your work within each chakra and how to pair them to maximise their potency.

- Create new boundaries that you honour every day, knowing others will honour them too, allowing your values and beliefs to be respected and your energy to be protected.
- Discover what I mean when I refer to myself as an Energy Alchemist and you as a Curious Creatrix.

The Answers You Seek

Sometimes when you are feeling low and out of alignment you stop trusting in yourself, but the quiet voice of intuition always lies inside of you.

You already know many of the answers you seek, it's just that when you don't slow down to listen – because you're trying so hard to force and direct your energy to where you think the answers lie, to where you think they *should* be – then often you can find that your questions are met with more questions. You can push all you want trying to fit that square peg into a round hole, but your energy will resist. It will know that this isn't the answer for you, or it isn't meant for you at this time, and it will find a way to push back, leaving you feeling drained, defeated or unmotivated.

By learning to stop trying to control all of the different elements and by releasing any attachment you hold to a specific outcome or timeframe, you can stop trying to push and force and allow for flow and ease, and you might just find you're taken effortlessly, exactly to the answers you need.

Energy just wants to be allowed to flow and transmute. When you submit to giving energy the freedom to flow, then transformations can happen in whatever way they need to.

You can begin to let go of habits, thought patterns, limiting beliefs and stories that weigh you down – negative energy is so heavy – and you can tap into the light energy that freely surrounds you.

Even during the times when your life seems easy-going and non-eventful you are still continuously picking up on other people's energy. Their moods, tone, attitudes and problems, this can be what drains you of your energy without you even realising it.

Sometimes energy work is a slow-burn work in progress that takes a lifetime to achieve. It takes time and deliberate effort to keep looking within, to keep being honest with yourself. It takes courage to make changes. Changes you may be hesitant to make right now, as current habits, beliefs and go-to reactions are holding you back. These may have all served a purpose for you at some time or other, but now they are more harmful than helpful.

Those things that once propelled you forwards are now what's keeping you stuck.

Sometimes energy work is as simple as taking a few well-timed breaths to breathe in the light energy and breathe out the heavy energy.

I invite you to try it now.

Inhale through your nose and exhale out of your mouth.

Breathe in a crystalline white light and breathe out any stagnant energy.

Breathe in and breathe out.

Breathe in and breathe out.

Breathe in and breathe out.

My wish for you is that you become able to:

- See yourself and your life as extraordinary, rather than ordinary.
- Alchemise from your and other people's expectations of who you *should* be, to who you *really* are.
- Free yourself from your fears, doubts, and limiting beliefs.

Because you have the potential to transform your life, to align your thoughts, feelings and actions with your beliefs and values to live within those standards. It is so important to know your boundaries, honour them and have others respect them too.

Existing in this soulful awareness is the ultimate transformation.

What I would like to share with you are strategies and life skills that are so very important but perhaps you were left to figure them out for yourself.

Perhaps no one taught you how important it is to get to know yourself.

To be able to calm your mind when mind monkeys occur or big decisions need to be made.

To like and, more importantly, still love yourself when you don't make the best choices and mistakes are made.

Knowing that you can change your entire perspective of everything you've ever been through and everything that's yet to come by changing the way you think, is very empowering.

Your mind is capable of so much more than just being used for survival, problem-solving and gaining knowledge. It is the most wonderful tool for being creative and for bringing joy and abundance into your life, and you do need to know how to bring that beautifully abundant energy into your life every day.

What Is Energy Alchemy?

What do I mean by the phrase 'energy alchemy' or when I call myself an Energy Alchemist? And what do I mean when I refer to you as a Curious Creatrix?

Let's look individually at the words energy, alchemist, curious and Creatrix:

- Energy is a single word to describe the ability to work. Batteries give your remote control the ability to work, just as electricity gives your kettle the ability to work.

- An alchemist is someone who takes something already good and transforms it for the better. They are people who see the wonder, magic and power of possibility in the world.

- Curious means being eager to learn or know something.

- A Creatrix is a woman deeply connected to herself. She co-creates with the universe, understanding there must be a balance in all things. She is powerful yet owns her vulnerability. She knows that there can be no light without the dark. She honours her cyclical nature and is ever-evolving, ever-changing, ever-seeking answers to rise into her feminine creative power. She unapologetically creates her own life without seeking external validation or permission. Everything she crafts shows her values, honesty, integrity and purpose.

As an Energy Alchemist, I help you take your ability to work and transform it for the better, so you too can see the wonder, magic and possibility in the world.

As a Curious Creatrix, you seek to learn how to step fully into your Creatrix power to create a life you love, unapologetically, as the protector of your own energy.

Working within the energy of the chakras, I want this alchemy to transform you from limiting beliefs, doubts and shadows to self-acceptance and 'this is who I am, unapologetically me'.

You have the potential to transform. To create a new vision for your future. To design a more aligned version of yourself, for yourself.

That's the really important part to remember, that what you are aiming to achieve here, the changes that you wish to make, are made by you, for you.

By you, because no one else can do the deep inner work on your behalf – it all has to be you.

For you, because this won't be aligned action if you're doing it for someone else.

When you live within the cycles of your energy, cleansing and balancing your chakras, you can align your thoughts, feelings, emotions, and actions.

You can then balance the energy between your mind and body, inner and outer world, your masculine and feminine, and your master and student path.

There will always be a little part of yourself that you keep tucked away just for you, and that is perfectly OK, but I want you to feel confident enough to show who you truly are to the world and to know that you are assured enough to process the world in a way that has meaning for you and gives you a sense of belonging.

Fight, Flight, Freeze & Fawn

Whenever you find you are not in energetic alignment there are 4 default states you work from: fight, flight, freeze and fawn.

Fight is being angry at the world for all of your problems.

- Anger
- The need to control
- A need to have all the answers
- Explosive outbursts
- Reactions and not responses
- Questioning everything because it all feels personal
- Why is this happening to me? Why now?

Flight is keeping yourself so busy that your thoughts don't have the time to catch up with you.

- Working hard so you don't have to work out what's wrong or what needs to change
- Being single task-focused
- Increased anxiety
- Inability to sit still
- Procrastination
- Perfectionism

Freeze is the inability to choose, in the hope that the problem will just roll along like a tumbleweed all by itself.

- If you stay still long enough then the issue will resolve itself
- You can't make decisions or you refuse to make decisions
- You feel stuck
- You isolate yourself

- You feel numb

Fawn is turning to others. Not for help but as a distraction, a way to feel useful.

- People pleasing
- Loss of identity
- No boundaries
- Overwhelm
- Becoming co-dependent
- Looking to help others because helping them is easier than helping yourself

All of these are different ways to attempt to turn off or shut out your thoughts. They are a form of avoidance tactics, but you already know that the things you leave unresolved come back to bite you later. The one thing that connects all of these very different states of being and silences your intuition, your inner voice, is your need for certainty.

Whenever anything unexpected or unwanted happens, you immediately look for the certainties – what do you know to be true about this situation?

Then you focus on needing the certainty of knowing exactly what comes next.

- How does this event play out?
- How long will this issue be in my life?
- What is the end result?
- What is the right decision to make?

But certainty is something that no one can ever offer you.

Rarely can you solely control or influence an outcome because it's never just you and the event that is happening; there are always other factors involved, other people involved. You can only control your part in the outcome, and this is a step-by-step process:

- Gather information
- Make an informed decision

- Act on your decision
- Reassess
- Repeat

Just like a board game, you move your piece around the board the best way you can to win the game. But you have no idea how the dice will fall or how other players will choose to move their pieces.

You can only ever make the choice that feels right for you at that moment with the knowledge that's available.

Of course, hindsight is going to afford you the realisation of knowing whether you made the right choices. But I believe if you did what was right for you, in each moment and at each step, then that's all that you could have done.

And then you get to store this knowledge, to recall it the next time you are in a similar situation, to guide you as to whether you make the same decision again or take a completely different approach.

This is my loving nudge to tune back into **you**.

Especially if right now you are feeling afraid, discouraged, stuck or wanting to make a change.

If right now you are in fight, flight, freeze or fawn mode.

I want you to feel at peace, to be able to trust in yourself and the decisions that you make.

My hope is that you take on board the information you will read here, take information that you can find for yourself elsewhere and take what resonates and leave what doesn't. The way that resonates is the one that feels good, lights you up inside and flows effortlessly.

This doesn't mean you get to avoid the difficult part, the shadow work, because that's the most important work that needs to be done.

But concerning how you approach and achieve making decisions, and the method you choose for letting go and forgiving, you can choose the way that feels the best for you. The way that feels right.

Once you have found your way then change becomes a positive, something to look forward to and not something to be feared or resisted.

Everything Is Energy

Energy governs so much of your day: your thoughts begin it, your emotions amplify it and your actions set it in motion.

When you are 100% charged and aligned nothing phases you. You live from a place of abundance, exuberance, gratitude and happiness. There is an openness and acceptance that things happen *for* you as an opportunity and not *to* you like a punishment for something you've done.

Everything is energy and that's all there is to it. Match the frequency of the reality you want and you cannot help but get that reality. It can be no other way.

This is not philosophy

This is physics – Albert Einstein

Energy is all around you, in everything you see, hear, touch, smell, taste, and do. It's in the way you carry yourself, the words you speak and the connection you have to others and with yourself.

4 Types of Energy & 7 Cups

There are 4 types of energy that you use and have access to every day:

- Physical – the energy required to complete your daily tasks.
- Mental – the energy required to problem solve, be creative and be organised.
- Emotional – the energy required to connect fully to friendships and relationships, and your ability to deal with all of life's ups and downs.
- Spiritual – the energy required to live with meaning and passion. Your source of inspiration and how you connect to everyone and everything you care about.

Underneath those 4 types of energy, there are 7 areas, or cups, in your life that you direct those 4 energies into.

I like to think of them as cups, as we have the word recuperation which means *to recover from illness or exertion*. Re-cup-eration: to refill those cups in order to recuperate.

You may choose to call them areas, pillars or containers, but for our time together I'll refer to them as cups.

These 7 cups are:

- Physical – your health and the need for activity and exercise. The need to nourish your body with healthy food and drink choices. The need for sleep to rest and recharge.
- Emotional – being able to cope effectively with life's ups and downs and creating satisfying relationships. Having the appropriate response to situations and events.
- Financial – being satisfied with both your current and future financial situations and goals.

- Environmental – maintaining good mental health by occupying a tidy, pleasant, stimulating, safe space; somewhere you thrive just by being there.
- Spiritual – expanding your sense of purpose, investigating what your beliefs and values are.
- Occupational/intellectual – enrichment from your chosen profession or the ability to further your knowledge in subjects that interest you.
- Social – feelings of connection and belonging. Having friendships that support you in times of need.

No wonder you get tired. You take the 4 energy sources you have access to and divide them over the 7 cups just mentioned, and that's just to keep you aligned. Then if you take into account all the name tags you have, all the names you respond to: mum, daughter, sister, employer, employee, aunt, friend and wife, to name but a few.

That's a lot of expelled energy in a day.

This is why understanding yourself as an energy being is so important.

Comparisonitis?

When you become depleted of energy, when you feel like you've nothing left to give, then you may have noticed how much easier it becomes to spend time looking outside of yourself. To study other people, to people watch. Social media grants you the ability to do this easily every day. Sometimes this leads to comparison, where it can feel like the life you lead isn't enough; you don't own enough, earn enough, have enough, do enough, and perhaps there are even feelings that you yourself are not enough. This causes you to want to do more, be more and buy more. But the result is that you move further away from what you were trying to achieve. Your level of comparison then increases and you begin to judge or perhaps envy others for what they appear to have and the life they lead. Judgement or envy over how they dress, how they handle their emotions, how they carry themselves around others, how they spend their time and money, and how effortless their lives appear to be.

When you allow yourself to constantly make these comparisons, your life against theirs, it makes it difficult to be honest with yourself, to look at the reality of your own life, to pause and be grateful for what you already have.

Have you ever stopped to think that perhaps it is your life that appears effortless to someone else? Perhaps right now, they envy you for something they perceive you have. Is there something you once wanted and now have, but in all of this comparison, you've forgotten how far you've already come? This outward-looking is a common tactic used when trying to suppress any feelings, emotions and occurrences you don't want to face or deal with. You switch to external looking, maybe even going into fix-it mode to help others, as helping someone else, immersing yourself in their life, is always an easier task than looking inwardly towards helping yourself.

You'll notice I said that envy or judgement is based on what others *appear* to have. This is because you never truly know what is going on in someone else's life, you don't know what daily battles they face. You don't know what kind of journey they have had to get to where they are now. In both real life and on social media only the best of yourself, the best of times, gets presented. The bad situations and the mistakes all remain hidden from view.

While you are comparing, be mindful of what stage of the journey someone else is at. Comparing parenting skills when you have a newborn and they have a teenager or comparing you at the beginning of a new career to someone who is 6 years in isn't even a fair comparison to begin with. Don't compare your chapter 3 to their chapter 10.

Yet maybe you're still sat with lots of thoughts looping around in your mind, looking to fix problems that aren't there. When you spend time, energy and effort on chasing every thought to see where it leads and while you're busy being busy, being all things to all people, wondering how your life stacks up against someone else's, then you slip further and further down your list of priorities, ending up overwhelmed, burnt out, exhausted and energetically out of alignment.

As you embark on this journey, I'm going to ask that you work on being completely honest with yourself. Be true to yourself, as that is where the magic of energy alchemy lies.

I want to encourage you to come down from your mind and into your body to enable you to stop overthinking, comparing, wondering, and doing, but rather just to breathe and be. You are a human being after all.

Embrace the connection between body and mind, physical and spiritual.

I ask that you now hold space for yourself, to affirm that you will allow comparison to turn to compassion.

I ask that you come into the essence of just being and belonging any time you need to. Not trying to fit into society, not trying to please all the people that surround you, not being everything to everyone, and not tied to any particular circumstance or event that currently keeps draining you of energy.

I welcome you to the process of rediscovery.

What Are Chakras?

Chakras are concentrated energy centres of the body, with each chakra corresponding to a different physical, emotional or spiritual state of being. They hold an influence over all areas of your life.

In Sanskrit, chakra means wheel or disc. Chakra energy moves in circles, not just inside you but around your whole being.

The energy that flows through the chakras may be known to you as Chi, Qi, Prana, life force energy, source energy, or something else.

The chakras allow this energy both in and out, as they are both receivers and transmitters.

Every moment of every day you pull in energy from those around you. Being with a happy person can raise your energy, just as being around someone having a difficult time can lower it.

Learning how to keep this energy moving through your chakra system prevents any stagnant energy from building up in your body. The more your energy is moved and purified, the more you can allow a better quality of energy to be received. The purification of energy happens automatically as you focus on moving the energy.

Looking after your mind and body by way of nutrition, exercise and being mindful of your thoughts, will all help to keep the energy moving and will encourage wonderful energy into your being.

Once you have cleared away the old energy you will become able to store the purified energy, and then your immune system becomes strengthened as this enhances your body's ability to heal.

This will give you more energy to utilise daily. No more starting the day from a half-empty battery.

Your thoughts, intentions, words, actions and responses will become charged with this aligned, abundant energy, allowing you a stronger influence over what comes into your life.

It's OK to retreat for a while to spend time intentionally noticing your chakras and your energy.

As you progress through this book you may feel like more than one chakra is out of alignment. This is because when one is blocked, the others try to compensate and become either under - or overactive.

It is important to find the right balance for you across these 7 chakras. Your balance won't look the same as someone else's and that's OK, it's not supposed to. Your own balance will even shift and evolve as priorities ebb and flow in and out of your life.

Your aim is to keep your chakras in a stable, receptive condition.

There are thought to be 114 chakras in total. Some people like to work on a 12-chakra system, whilst others prefer to work on a 7-chakra system.

The 12-chakra system includes the 7 primary chakras that reside inside the body, plus a further 5 chakras that lie outside the body.

I will be concentrating on the 7 primary chakras that lie inside your body.

These are:

- Root
- Sacral
- Solar plexus
- Heart
- Throat
- Brow
- Crown

Close your eyes, open your mind,

all the answers you seek, you can find.

When you balance your chakras, root to crown,

you transmute everything that weighs you down.

Root is the Earth and the seeds you will sow,

sacral, your feelings, and how you will grow.

Solar plexus is your place of personal power,

heart is your love that unfurls like a flower.

Throat is I speak, all the words that you say,

brow your intuition, gaining strength every day.

Crown is for actioning all that you know,

empowered and wise through your life you now go.

You've raised your vibration and cleared your mind,

the answers you seek, you will easily find.

You're a Curious Creatrix, whose dreams can come true,

go create your life with all that you wish to be, have, and do.

Lynsey Limb

Root Chakra

The root chakra or Muladhara: I am.

Situated at the base of the spine.

Represented by the colour red.

Physical symptoms of imbalance include restlessness, the inability to sit still, making unhealthy eating choices, cramps, fatigue and lethargy.

You can help to keep this area balanced by cleaning the house, spending time in nature, sitting on the ground, walking barefoot, dancing or cooking.

When this area is balanced, you feel alive and free, optimistic and full of vitality. You feel safe, secure, centred, grounded, happy to be alive with a seize-the-day outlook.

If there is too much energy here, it can trigger feelings of selfishness and of being overbearing, there is greed for more, a lust for power and you may be more materialistic than usual.

If too little energy flows here then you may experience feelings of being unlikable, unloved or that you just don't fit in. There may be an inability to complete tasks for feelings of anxiousness, fear or doubt. You will be unsure of your financial situation, with a feeling of unease.

As previously mentioned, you have 7 cups that you fill with the 4 energies available to you, but at the side of those cups sits a big old leaky bucket.

This is a place where energy flows out the bottom as fast as you pour it in. These are all the areas that you focus on a lot but aren't worthy of your time. All of the procrastinating, comparing, wondering and those negative thoughts you keep going over in your mind. It's also those jobs you know you have to do but don't want to do.

Unfortunately, you can't plug that bucket up entirely, as there will always be some energy that goes into it, but you can make sure you are very aware and mindful of exactly what is going in the bucket.

If you find that a particular activity or task drains you and you know you don't have a choice about whether you complete it or not, then you can choose to do something afterwards that you know you do enjoy, to reset your balance and to refill one of your cups.

I encourage you to write a nourish list.

Write down all the things that you enjoy. Things that instantly either relax you or leave you feeling re-energised.

This is now your go-to list of activities to do to reset the balance after a leaky bucket kind of day.

This is the time to begin a new habit.

A healthy habit.

~

The base or root is where you nurture your development. The desire to feel stable and secure with the knowledge that you have everything you need to thrive, lie here.

As you are reading this now, I would like you to imagine a flowering indoor plant. Notice all its healthy green leaves, admire the flowers it has produced, vibrant in colour. Wonder if they hold a scent.

Now picture beneath to the parts you can't see, to the soil and the roots. Not nearly as pretty as the visible parts but vital for the plant's survival. Without its long strong roots, the plant could not take nourishment from the earth and could not grow and flourish.

You are just the same as this plant, and it's through your base chakra you gain knowledge, self-realisation, and the ability to set boundaries that enable you to grow your own strong roots. These will allow you to grow, flourish, nourish yourself and hold steady in a storm.

Here in the soil of the root chakra, you can plant seeds. Ideas of things you would like to have, like to do, like to change, and the person you wish to be.

It is here you are reminded that you are just as responsible for what you choose *not* to do, as well as that which you choose *to* do. Inaction is still action and not choosing is still a choice. Be sure that you are setting the right intentions and remove self-doubts and beliefs that are not your own. It is amazing how many beliefs you may currently hold that are not your own because, fully or in part, they came with you from childhood. You still automatically believe in the things you were told as a child without now pausing to check to see if they're still actually your beliefs today.

They also stem from your desire to be accepted by those closest to you, so when you are with loved ones and good friends, the people you spend the most time with, their traits, behaviours and beliefs can be mimicked subconsciously by you so that you can mirror them to fit in.

The more clarity you have over who you are, what you need to thrive, what beliefs you truly hold for yourself, then the more you can be aware of areas you wish to change.

You have to get rid of old beliefs in order to make way for the new.

Here in the root chakra, you are asked to forgive yourself for any mistakes from your past, as they will have brought lessons with them. When you choose to learn the lesson rather than to dwell on any negative feelings, emotions, outcomes or regrets, then you gain strength and become better prepared to be able to cope with future similar life experiences.

Any time your mind turns to overthinking about lack, regret or those feelings of not being enough or not being worthy, then your self-talk becomes negative and this drains you very quickly of your energy. It is important to give up the well-worn thought programmes, the stories that you tell yourself over and over: *I'm not good enough, I'll be happier when* or *I've tried to make changes in the past but I just can't.*

When you learn to switch these off, it makes way for kinder self-talk and more positive, healthier ways of thinking.

Treat yourself the same way you would treat your best friend.

Show yourself empathy, kindness and compassion.

Speak to yourself in a kindly manner.

It's difficult to grow and flourish if someone is being mean to you all the time. It's even more difficult if that someone being mean is you.

You are enough exactly as you are.

I'd like you to take some time now to ask yourself:

- What is it I want to do?
- What seeds am I going to be planting?

- What boundaries do I need to have in place to protect my energy?
- What is something that would increase my feelings of being able to achieve these goals?

Here, in your root, lies the blueprint for all that you came here to be, do and have.

As a child, you probably had a hobby or activity that you loved to do.

Something that was effortless and made you happy. You could do this thing over and over again and never grow tired of it.

What was it that you were good at and loved doing?

I ask because I'm curious: when was the last time that you felt that carefree and wild?

Doing something purely because you wanted to, because it made you feel happy and free.

The answer should come quickly to you. It might be a proper memory or just a flicker of a thought, but your heart will remember. It could seem so simple or even perhaps silly that you might at first dismiss it, but hold on to that thought and explore it a little further because whatever just came to mind, that is your talent, your passion That is what lies at the root of you.

Don't ignore those early talents and suppress them. Don't hide them from the world, as this is something only you can do. Others may, of course, do something similar but don't let that put you off, as no one else can do it in the same way as you, not with the same passion, creativity, intention, reason, energy or voice as you.

If you already still do this activity, either as a career or as a hobby, then just be reminded now of your why. Why is it that you do this? In what way does it enrich your life?

If this is something you no longer do then why not?

Were you told you shouldn't, couldn't, or mustn't? Was it deemed to not be a real career choice?

Did you just stop doing it naturally as other interests and pursuits occurred?

If the activity has lain dormant since childhood, then look to guide it back into your life in some way. If that specific activity is no longer possible, then just remember what feelings and emotions it evoked for you. What was your why? Then think about other activities that feel effortless and bring you the same joy and elation. Encourage more of that into your life.

Sit now in the sense of being safe and secure, grounded and supported in what you really, passionately want to do.

It's time to dissolve the blocks and the fears you currently have, to plant the seeds of who you want to be. The version of you, you know you are destined to be.

I want you to be able to set yourself boundaries, to know what you are available for and what you are now no longer available for. To find the words to speak up and to live unapologetically within these standards that you are creating for yourself.

Sacral Chakra

Sacral chakra or Svadhisthana: I feel.

Situated 5cm below your belly button.

Represented by the colour orange.

Physical symptoms of imbalance include lower back pain or stiffness, urinary issues or kidney pain.

You can help to keep this area balanced by spending time at the water: oceans, lakes, rivers, going for a swim, or simply bathe or shower. Moonlight is especially energising for this chakra.

When this chakra is balanced there is passion, creativity, good health, optimism and openness to new ideas. You feel friendly, your imagination is at its best and you can focus on objectives. You show concern for others, you have tolerance, patience and you wholeheartedly trust your intuition. You also have the ability to look inwardly at your successes and failures, to focus on future ambitions.

If this area is overactive, you can feel over-emotional, manipulative, there are feelings of not working properly. Feelings of guilt that perhaps lead to an excess of food, sex or alcohol. You pleasure seek as you feel self-centred. You become overly ambitious, even jealous or distrusting.

If too little energy flows here then there may be low libido or shying away from intimacy. You may feel you lack creativity as you feel isolated, shy, and hypersensitive, with a confused and aimless feeling to life.

This is the area of your desires, your source of inspiration and creativity. It affects your ability to feel emotions and sensations, and controls your ability to let go of stored emotions from the past. It heavily influences your sexuality, sexual love, open-mindedness and your ability to cooperate with others.

Anger – Jealousy – Cruelty – Hate – Greed – Laziness.

How do you feel as you read those words?

These are 6 emotions that can raise very different feelings.

Quite naturally, these probably aren't your go-to everyday emotions. You don't actively seek to feel angry, you don't look for ways to be cruel on purpose and you aren't by nature hateful, but still, at some point, you will have felt some, if not all, of these.

Perhaps sometimes you get caught up remembering a time you experienced:

- Anger: you may have spoken harshly in the heat of the moment then regretted it immediately and ever since.

- Hate: hating a certain circumstance that came out of nowhere and knocked you for six.

- Greed: a time when you experienced lack and wanted more of something.

- Jealousy: feeling despondent, as everyone else seemed to have it better or easier than you.
- Cruelty: causing someone else discomfort because you felt powerless in your own situation.
- Laziness: that feeling that you should be busy being busy all the time, and that time spent doing nothing is frowned upon.

And I'm sure there are times when you were on the receiving end of others as they experienced those emotions.

Understanding, forgiveness, empathy and kindness both towards yourself and others are what will help you here. When you gain the ability to put yourself in another person's shoes, then you can see their perspective and take the time to respond rather than react. You can then calm your emotions, which in turn lead to your feelings, before they take over and consume you.

Connecting to all of your emotions, even the ones you see as negative, is very energetically empowering.

All emotions are valid and are there to be felt.

Emotions, feelings and moods come and go. They don't define you; they're just a part of your day for a little while and then they dissipate.

Acceptance is the key word here: to accept all emotions, feelings and moods without the need to judge them. It's OK to sit with them for a while, to really notice them, investigate them, and recognise what event raised them for you. You can sit with them and realise that you don't have to react to them. You can understand them and then respond to them.

Here's a little something for you to remember the next time an emotion or feeling runs away with you.

R. A. I. N.

R. Recognise the feeling or emotion and what caused it.

A. Allow yourself to sit with it.

I. Investigate with kindness how it feels, no judgement.

N. Non-identify with the feeling. Remember you are not your feelings and emotions, so a bad word or a bad thought, a bad mood or a bad day, doesn't mean you are a bad person or that somehow you are predestined to have a bad life.

If you were carrying a full cup of coffee and you tripped over something, your coffee would most likely be spilled. There would be frustration that you hadn't seen the object, frustration at whoever left the object there, frustration at having to clear up the mess and at having lost the drink you were looking forward to.

If I asked you why the coffee got spilled you would most likely reply that it was spilled because you tripped over, but in fact, it spilled simply because there was coffee in the cup.

If you had already enjoyed your drink and were heading back to the kitchen when the accident happened, you would have still tripped, you would have still lost your balance, the cup would have still tipped and the same laws of gravity would still apply, except that no coffee would have been spilled, as the cup was already empty.

This is the same for all of your feelings and emotions; perhaps in the heat of the moment you have said, done or thought something that you've later regretted, but you only did this because those emotions and feelings were there to be accessed.

~

I'd like you to call to mind a circle. This represents the connection that exists between yourself and others. Every day you connect in some way to the people that surround you: family and friends, colleagues, strangers, and even those you feel you dislike.

How do you connect your being to those around you?

How important are those connections to you?

Breathe in, now, an orange-coloured energy and wait for the circle to become clearer and sharper. Imagine it has a reflective surface like a pool or a mirror. You are going to look inside to see what happens there for you on the level of sacral energy. When you think about your connection to others, which connection immediately enters your mind?

Hold the image of this person in your mind. Think about your connection with them, and take a moment to feel gratitude that they are in your life.

When choosing this person, your thoughts will have, no doubt, turned to those you love. Perhaps this is someone you see daily and can help them when they ask, or perhaps your loved one is further away and you don't see them as much as you would like to and spend time wishing they were closer.

Take a moment to really feel your connection to this person, to tell them what they mean to you. Just have this conversation in your mind. Let your heart fill with gratitude and your sacral glow with joy at having such a beautiful and meaningful connection.

To everyone in your life that you love, you give a little of yourself to them. Sometimes you give away so much energy that you drain your reserves. You repeatedly put others before yourself.

You cannot pour from an empty cup, as the saying goes.

Picture before you a desert. Dry, hot sand everywhere you look. This signifies you if you become so busy and keep giving to others or trying to please others, that you forget to take the time to water the beautiful plant that is you. The plant that is your very foundation. Now all there is, is sand. It is time to stop giving your all to others. It is time to refocus back on yourself, not because you are being selfish, but because you have ignored yourself to the point that your emotional, physical, mental and spiritual energies are drained. You are now a desert.

You live in a world where there is a constant exchange of energy; there are times when you give and there are times when it is your turn to receive. Life would be unfair if you were only ever able to give or only ever able to receive. So if you are a natural giver, you need to notice when it is time to stop and allow yourself your turn to receive without any guilt, shame, blame or any other negative emotions you may associate with your sense of self.

It is OK to acknowledge that you need to learn to love yourself more. You are allowed a place on your to-do list.

You're not saying me first, you're saying me too.

Your sacral energy needs to be nourished and treated with gentleness and kindness, so send an orange light out into the room until it becomes filled with a warm, orange, loving glow.

As you sit in the charge of this orange sacral energy, release the ideas that you may have carried over from your childhood that say you need to wait.

Wait for someone else to love you, to look after you, to give you what you need. To wait for the good times, the better times. To wait for permission to stop or start something. Because that may have been true when you were little, but as an adult no one apart from you will ever know honestly, totally and absolutely what you need. Only you are the expert of you.

You no longer have to wait.

The time is right when *you* decide it is.

You can permit yourself to change what you feel needs to be changed whenever you like.

You are a self-maintaining being, and it is OK to rely on yourself to supply your own needs, goals and desires. You may, of course, need extra help or support at times, and it's important to recognise when that is, to ask for help when you truly need it and not allow yourself to sit and struggle. But your main power is in your ability to be self-sufficient enough to not be reliant on anyone to provide validation and support for you daily.

Then when you enter into a relationship whether that is a new friendship or a romantic partner, they are adding to what you are already able to provide for yourself.

I encourage you to embrace yourself and vow to love yourself utterly and completely, accepting yourself as you are inside and out, and begin to release comparison, guilt, blame, shame, regret and any other emotions that drain you of your energy.

Solar Plexus Chakra

Solar plexus or Manipura: I do/I become.

Situated 2cm above your tummy button in line with the bottom of your rib cage.

Represented by the colour yellow.

Physical symptoms of imbalance include nausea, digestive problems, nerve pain and issues with the liver or kidneys.

You can help to keep this area balanced by spending more time outdoors in the sunshine or by practising the sun salutation yoga sequence.

When this chakra is balanced you feel confident and in control. You are aware of your personal power. You feel driven, happy, free of self-doubt, and have the ability to organise. You pause to enjoy your accomplishments and all that is going well for you.

If the energy in this area is overactive, anger rises easily; you become power-hungry, domineering and a perfectionist – highly critical of yourself and others.

If too little energy lies here, then everything seems complicated, everything feels like an uphill battle. You may feel that others place too many demands on you, you will have low self-esteem, feelings of powerlessness, and an inferiority complex.

Being aware of an imbalance here is so important, as this highlights just how well you know yourself.

This chakra allows you to pick up on the vibrational energy from people, places and objects around you. It is the home of your personal power, self-control, emotions and feelings surrounding self-acceptance.

This is where you find clarity, self-confidence and well-being. Here you hold respect and understanding, empathy and sympathy.

The solar plexus allows you to achieve what you want from life and to enjoy those achievements once they have occurred.

You can use your power to manifest, to call in prosperity and balance. This allows you to feel safe and secure.

If your solar plexus is fully charged you are better equipped to deal with changes, as you will take the time to see if they lead to something better.

Minute by minute you have the power of choice. The power to choose your mindset, words, attitude, approach, behaviour, responses and habits and, therefore, how you interact with everyone and everything in your life.

As you sit here in the space of the solar plexus, know that it is supported by the previous 2 chakras, root and sacral, as you continue to heal and move any stagnant energy. You are continually growing roots and rediscovering yourself through every breath you take and every decision you make.

~

Going through your everyday life it can feel like you're inside a hamster wheel. All of your energetic investments – the effort, the hard work, all of the giving, planning and doing – it all seems never-ending. Using so much of your energy but never quite seeing the results you desire. Struggling with a list of never-ending tasks that don't seem to get completed, no matter what you do or how hard you try.

Two great exercises to help you here are:

1. Change your mindset to one of gratitude, by switching from I *have* to do this job, to I *get* to do this job.

2. Reframe your to-do list into a ta-dah list.

Instead of seeing another pile of laundry, which makes you inwardly groan and wonder if someone lives with you that you haven't met yet because you can't understand where it all comes from, you can express gratitude for the fact that you have clothes that need washing and a machine to wash them in.

Instead of seeing the dishes as a chore, there's gratitude for having had delicious food to eat.

Then, secondly, you can begin to see your to-do list as a permanent working document, something that can never be completed, as there will always be things that need to go on that list.

If you take out the emotion behind the list and all the unnecessary pressure you put on yourself to complete as much as possible in as short a time as possible, then you will just see it as a list.

By beginning a ta-dah list instead, you write down all that you did accomplish.

To begin with, you may choose to write out everything:

Got out of bed.

Took a shower

Made breakfast

And then at the end of the day, rather than looking at a list of things you didn't quite get around to, you have a list of positivity, a list of your accomplishments.

~

Do you ever feel stuck? Like Groundhog Day, life is the same, day after day. Perhaps you're going through the motions, doing all the things and taking all the action but nothing much is happening. Maybe you feel so stuck you're in freeze mode and have stopped even trying to do anything to alter your circumstances. Or perhaps you feel lonely. You're surrounded by people but still feel isolated and like there is no one to turn to.

You are neither stuck nor alone, even though sometimes I know it can feel that way.

If you were to replay the last few weeks, you might notice that there was interaction with someone. Whether it was somebody kind to you in the street or someone stopping to greet you good morning.

Maybe you started a day feeling overtired and a little tetchy, and suddenly somebody just smiled at you. Perhaps you received a surprise: a present, a token of gratitude or recognition for something well done.

Life reminds you, often, that you're not alone and you're not stuck. You are always part of one large existence that's constantly moving, evolving and changing.

Sometimes, when you feel stuck or alone it's because of your mind. It works by repeatedly bringing up an experience over and over again until you reach an outcome you deem acceptable. You label events as good or bad, right or wrong, so that you can efficiently process the right and the good and store them neatly away in your mind. Then you endlessly replay the bad and the wrong and all of their subsequent outcomes, leaving you pondering over all the things you could have said or done differently.

This is what keeps you trapped in that cycle.

If you break the habit of repeatedly thinking those same thoughts and accept that the past can't be changed, then you can just observe what you're doing now. Where are you now? Who is with you now? What is happening now? You will see that even if something feels the same, there is a change from the last time you were in a similar situation. Every day, moment by moment, there is some form of subtle change. An event brings about a different emotion, or a situation leads to a different outcome. A decision ends in a different choice. Each time you encounter an experience, even though it feels the same, there will be some slight variation to it.

There will be a variation because there has been growth. You will have learned something from the last time you were in a similar situation. Subconsciously, these small changes manifest bigger changes, and these bigger changes mean that you will change.

Without a balanced third chakra, you can feel stuck in a passive life, wading through treacle and going through the motions, feeling like others have more control over your life than you do. Your third chakra allows for action, doing, changing, evolving, becoming.

You're not stuck. You are just committed to certain patterns of behaviour because they helped you in the past. Now those behaviours have become more harmful than helpful. The reason why you can't move forward is that you keep applying an old formula to a new level in your life. If you change the formula, you will get a different result – Emily Maroutian

You can rise from anything. You can completely recreate yourself. Nothing is permanent.

You are not stuck. You are not broken. You are not powerless.

You have choices, always.

You can think new thoughts, learn new behaviours, and create new habits or obtain new knowledge, any time you want.

All that matters is that you decide to make a change, be consistent in making that change happen and never look back.

~

Imagine that there is a fire before you and to the side is a stack of wooden sticks on which you can write. Take a stick and write a word or sentence representing something in your life that is no longer serving you in the way it once did.

Something you wish to release or let go of.

Remember that some things need to be let go of hundreds of times before you're truly free of them. Forgive yourself this process and allow it to take the time required: letting go is one of the hardest things for your mind to engage with.

Once you have written on the stick, place it into the flame and watch as it catches fire. Do this with as many sticks as you need to. As the last stick burns completely, a gust of wind blows and carries all the ash away from you.

After burning all of your sticks ask yourself:

- *Do I now have the energy to commit to all the things I wish to do?*
- *Do I feel lighter for this release?*
- *Do I now have more confidence?*
- *Am I clearer on what stands before me?*
- *Do I know what needs to change?*

You are powerful beyond measure and you can change any part of your life that you wish to change, any time that you want to.

Heart Chakra

Heart chakra or Anahata: I love.

Situated at the centre of the chest.

Represented by the colours green and light pink.

Physical symptoms of imbalance include high blood pressure, asthma or other respiratory issues, stiff joints, or problems with the hands.

To keep this area balanced wear something that incorporates pink or green, listen to music that makes you want to dance or sing.

When this chakra is in balance, you strike a personal balance that allows for unconditional love – this allows you to help others. There is peace within yourself as you feel loving, compassionate, tolerant, warm and open.

If this area is overactive then there are negative influences. You may feel unloved, feel more suspicious and repress your true emotions, thoughts and feelings. You will be jealous and codependent.

If there is too little energy here then this leads to a lack of empathy. There is bitterness, resentfulness, trust issues and intolerance.

I would love for this to be the shortest chapter I write in this book.

It would simply read.

Find people to love, who love you back equally and without condition.

Find the people who make your soul dance and your heart feel light.

See the world through the lens of gratitude and love.

Enjoy everything and everyone.

Laugh lots, love deeply.

The End

But the heart chakra is as complex as it is simple, and so this could easily be the longest chapter I write.

You desire to love and be loved. To be accepted exactly as you are without watering down any part of beautifully unique you.

Not wondering where you fit in, not having to mould yourself, to bend and give in to society's expectations of what is acceptable.

You require someone who can love you for you. All the quirkiness, kookiness, and being perfectly imperfect and just right for them. And by the same token, you want people in your life you can love in the same way.

You want to love freely and without conditions. You want an abundant, open, easy, carefree way of living where you don't have to hide any aspect of yourself.

You use your heart as a place to make decisions from. You may have spoken before about having to choose between your head or your heart when you were making a decision, but sometimes you're not choosing between your head and your heart at all, but rather between the 2 different sides of your heart. Here in the heart space lie both masculine and feminine energy; it is the only chakra to hold both.

All matters of the heart are dealt with and decided here but some of those decisions take longer to reach than others.

I love pizza. A matter-of-fact statement straight from your masculine energy. Words that you have no problem expressing.

I love you. A romantic statement from your feminine energy. There is the worry of rejection, and so these words may remain unsaid.

The masculine energy here in the heart is all about facts, logic and proof.

The feminine energy leans into what feels good but also holds a memory of past hurts and worries about being hurt again. It is also the power behind your belief. It's what encourages you to learn to trust again and to want to give those second chances.

This is why it is so important to have boundaries.

It is also important to distinguish between walls and boundaries.

Walls are very masculine in energy. They are something you build brick by brick around your heart in an effort to protect it. Impenetrable. Nothing in, nothing out. There's a reason and logic to building it.

This isn't a long-term solution though, as over time that protection turns to isolation and that in turn becomes loneliness. As a human you like and enjoy the company of others. You weren't designed to be alone for long periods; you were designed to be in groups, to be sociable, and share your experiences and your life with others.

Whilst walls might seem to offer protection, they also keep out all the joy in the world and the connection that you desire.

It might feel like it's a good thing to hold back your feelings but there is so much joy to be found in giving and receiving love.

Compassion, love, laughter, forgiveness, acceptance, gratitude, empathy, generosity, kindness, optimism and hope.

That's a lot to miss out on in this world if you keep those walls intact.

Boundaries are more fluid and feminine by nature. They don't mean you won't ever get hurt again, but you do have something in place by way of protection because if you really know yourself, trust your intuition and honour your boundaries, then your chance of getting hurt and misplacing your loyalty is lessened.

The right boundaries will see you with the confidence to believe in yourself and to trust.

Trust both yourself and others.

When you truly love there is a truth that you can't quantify or put into words. No logic can help you understand it; there is just a deep knowledge of its truth.

Here is a place where there may be a lot of shadow work to do. Lots of forgiving the past. It can't be changed, and so bringing all the hurt forwards with you only serves to hurt you more.

The 3 lower chakras – root, sacral and solar plexus – relate to personal energy, and the 3 higher chakras – throat, brow and crown – relate to collective power. The heart chakra lies in the centre and is the connection between physical and spiritual.

This chakra is where the other 6 meet, driven by love and influencing forgiveness, compassion, empathy, trust, balance, and a connection with nature.

It aids rejuvenation, rebirth, success, growth, prosperity and development.

~

There have been many versions of you during your life so far, and all of those versions still hold space inside of you; they have learned to evolve as you have grown older. They have changed and adapted throughout your life. They have each had their own experiences, and they each have their own story to tell. They all had a part to play in helping shape who you are today. All of their memories still exist in your mind. Their hurts are still your hurts, and their successes are still your successes.

All of those past versions of you are still wanting to be loved, acknowledged, listened to, appreciated and supported, especially if mistakes were made. One of them is maybe catching your eye again and again. Which version of you is it? How old were you then? What happened? What does that aspect of yourself need? Speak to them, let them know it's all OK. Forgive yourself for any mistakes.

Tell them how much you appreciate, honour and respect them, how proud you are of them. Especially remember all of the achievements, the good decisions, and all the fun times.

You can't go back and alter the past, but you can free yourself of the burden of bringing anger, resentment, bitterness, regret, and sorrow into the present version of you.

Give yourself permission to leave those negative emotions and feelings behind and move forward with a clean slate. Bring with you what you learned so that the same mistakes are not repeated. But it's time now to let the past be in the past. Let go of that which no longer serves you. Be free.

Look into a mirror as you repeat 3 times:

- *I'm sorry.*
- *Please forgive me.*

- *Thank you.*
- *I love you.*

Send that love, gratitude and forgiveness to all past versions of yourself to heal all past hurts.

The heart chakra is all about connection and relationships, about both giving and receiving love, and about how open you are in relationships.

Love is an important part of any relationship, whether that relationship is platonic, romantic, with others, or with yourself.

When you are open, receptive and balanced in this area, you can truly see all of life's beauty.

Throat Chakra

Throat chakra or Vishuddha: I speak.

Situated at the throat.

Represented by the colour blue.

Physical symptoms of imbalance include stiff neck, sore shoulders, sore throat, earaches or dental pain.

You can help to keep this chakra balanced by listening to music that energises you, by singing, looking at the sky, meditating outside, journaling and practising breathwork.

When this chakra is balanced you freely communicate, you feel centred, happy, confident, expressive, creative, tactful and diplomatic.

If your throat chakra is overactive, you may experience a lack of control over what you say. You may talk too much or without a filter. When the throat chakra is overwhelmed with energy you can become overly judgemental, and you may be quick to criticise. You may experience struggles in your relationships because of the harsh way you communicate. You may even become gossipy, rude or have the inability to listen.

If there is too little energy residing here then this results in you feeling nervous, frightened, introverted and insecure. There is a fear of speaking out, and if you try it results in a small, timid voice.

Sticks and stones may break my bones but words can never hurt me has to be the most inaccurate childhood rhyme I know. The power of words, whether written or spoken can lift you up or tear you down. Leave you crying with laughter or just crying.

They allow for you to speak your truth; it's how you share your thoughts, ideas, feelings, needs and desires.

They also allow you to express doubts, reservations, and fears.

Sometimes you may talk a lot but say very little, meaning you're happy to chat pleasantries and to pass the time of day but when asked the deeper questions, like how you are doing or feeling, you may answer with a simple *fine*.

When you have things on your mind, I know that sometimes it feels like a burden to offload to someone else. You may be mindful of things going on in their life and may not be sure if it's right to pour your heart out at that particular moment, but I believe a problem shared is a problem halved. If the person asking is a good friend or relative and has your best interests at heart, they will be asking because they genuinely care and want to know how you are. They want to help you if they can. Sometimes just having someone in your corner to listen makes your worries seem reduced.

~

Every time, before you share words, whether written or spoken, THINK.

T. Is it true? Repeating things that you hear without checking facts can be upsetting for all involved.

H. Is it helpful? Is what you are about to say going to help the person hearing it? If it's a form of feedback, it can still be done in a polite, tactful, diplomatic way. It doesn't have to be rude or blunt.

I. Is it inspiring? Will what you say encourage someone in some way? Will it inspire them to take a leap of faith or make a positive change?

N. Is it necessary? It's very common to feel uncomfortable with silence, so is what you're about to say necessary or is it just to fill a void?

K. Is it kind? If you always speak from the heart with a will to help others then you will always be working from a place of kindness, empathy and understanding.

Use your words for good. Let them be to share knowledge, to educate, inspire and motivate. If someone has done something for you recently that you are grateful for, then take the time to thank them personally. Take them out for coffee or phone them up to have a conversation to say thank you. You will both benefit from the exchange.

~

Your dreams, desires or goals all start with an idea, something that percolates in your mind for a while, but to make it feel real and like it could be achieved, you talk it through with someone. Then it has become attainable and you feel more accountable for making it happen.

Speaking your words out loud or seeing them written down gives you focus as you can't ignore them once you have shared them with others. This gives you the motivation to bring them to life.

Start with where you are now and then look at where you want to be. What steps need to happen for you to get from here to there?

If you need help from someone else, who do you need to ask?

What exactly will you ask for?

Whenever you are speaking, take the time to choose your vocabulary wisely.

Try to avoid over-apologising.

No more speaking in the negative; it's time to reframe your words to use positive language instead.

Save sorry for when you truly regret words, actions or deeds.

I'm sorry I'm late becomes *Thank you for waiting.*

Sorry that I talked too much becomes *Thank you for taking the time to listen, I appreciate it.*

I'm sorry that I have needed you so much lately becomes *Thank you for being a good person and looking out for me.*

Sorry, I don't seem to be very good at this becomes *Thank you for showing me patience while I learn.*

Sorry I'm so snappy at the moment becomes *Thank you for accepting me in my current mood.*

When you reframe in this way it keeps your energy positive. You're displaying gratitude and appreciation for others.

Sometimes though you do need to be able to say what is on your mind, so do permit yourself to say what you need to say, because when you keep swallowing words down it just leads to resentment eventually.

Don't just assume that people know what you're thinking or that it should be obvious. It is obvious to you as they are your thoughts and feelings and no doubt you've been brooding on them for a while, but if you don't verbalise your issue, then no one will know to help you.

When you verbalise, be specific!

If you need someone to stop doing something or start doing something then don't be afraid to ask outright for what you seek.

People like clear direction, so ask for what you need and state the time frame it should be completed by.

You'll get much better results, as everyone will know exactly what is expected and there will be no surprises or crossed wires.

Brow Chakra

Brow/third eye chakra or Ajna: I see.

Situated in the middle of the forehead between the eyebrows.

Represented by the colour indigo.

Physical symptoms of imbalance include vision problems, headaches, insomnia or nightmares.

You can help to keep this area balanced by looking at the night time sky or visualising the colour indigo.

When this chakra is balanced you feel in control of your life. You can identify your needs and feel confident in your abilities without the need to look to others to help you feel whole. Your sixth sense, or intuition, guides you well. You feel balanced, imaginative, intuitive with clear thoughts, and can see other people's points of view and that bigger picture.

When this chakra is overactive then there is a lack of concentration, making life confusing. You may have disturbed sleep or nightmares and may obsessively read into things that aren't there.

If too little energy flows here then there can be poor judgement, lack of focus and poor imagination. You can't see beyond your own beliefs or particular point of view. You will lack energy, feel disordered, unassertive, frightened of achieving, and be too sensitive to the feelings of others.

The brow chakra allows you to picture what has not yet come into being. It is the base of your intuition. It is your link to your imagination that allows you to dream, visualise, concentrate, to have insight and finely tuned awareness.

Every day you have access to guidance and information given by many external sources, but just how do you decide who you allow to give you direction and advice? How do you know whose instructions you should follow? How do you decide what knowledge to take forward with you and what to dismiss?

Your gut feeling or intuition is your guide here.

You need an open consciousness and a mind free of thoughts in order to see the truth.

It is here that you can bring your daydreams, desires and wildest dreams to life.

I bet you currently have some aspirations that you're working at manifesting:

- *I want/need/desire/dream about having …*
- *So that I can …*

Write them out so that you can see them. Write out as many as you like. Short, medium and long-term goals. They should be something that feels right for you at this moment, remembering that they will inevitably change along the way.

as you either bring them to life or they alter to flow with the situations and circumstances in your life.

They will change because you as a person will change. The people in your life, your life focus and your goals will change. Different decades all bring different life requirements, hopes, dreams and aspirations.

For now, set yourself one goal, dream or desire that you can manifest in a short time. Think about something you would like to achieve and your reason why. What will having this bring to your life?

Now focus all of your efforts, conversations, words, actions, deeds, and energy towards this one goal.

If ideas don't come to mind easily for you then try the perfect day exercise below.

If you were just you, with no work ties or family commitments, no time constraints or money worries, what would your ideal day look like from start to finish?

Where would you be?

What would you be doing?

Who would you be with?

What would you wear?

What would you eat?

What would you spend your time doing?

Be very detailed and specific.

Take one part of that perfect day that you can bring into reality over the next month, and use that as your current aim.

~

As an adult, you have many different roles that you undertake or nametags that you wear, perhaps mum, aunt, daughter, granddaughter, niece, friend, sister, employee, employer or carer. Your words and behaviour won't be the same across all of these roles.

Your choice of words or the aspect of self you share will be different with friends than it is with your partner and the way you interact with your partner won't be the same as the way you interact with your parents or children.

You adapt and modify yourself according to who you are with at the time. Here lie your limiting beliefs about who you believe yourself to be within these roles. Who you think you *should* be versus who you are *destined* to be, if only you could just trust your intuition and follow your inner guidance.

As I mentioned in the heart chakra chapter, there are 2 types of energy that you work from daily: masculine and feminine. Both of these energies reside inside everyone and are responsible for things like logic and control, creative thinking and flow.

Masculine energy is analytical, competitive, single task-focused, rational, determined, linear and logical, objective, assertive, goal-oriented, forgetful, outward-looking, aware of the mind, a risk-taker.

Feminine energy is intuitive, collaborative, able to multitask, emotional, passionate, creative, empathetic, receptive, it allows for flow, it remembers, it is inward-looking, aware of all senses, a nurturer.

Sometimes you are ruled more by your masculine energy, that need for deadlines, blueprints, linear and logic, so you need to actively give yourself permission to access your feminine energy, to just take a breath and allow for things to happen naturally without all the push and hustle and busyness.

Think of your intuition as a muscle: regular exercise of it and paying attention to it will strengthen it.

I'm sure there have been times when you have been somewhere new or been introduced to someone you have never met and it just felt right. The place felt like home or the person felt like meeting a long-lost friend where the conversation just flowed and the laughter came easily.

By the same token, upon being somewhere new or meeting someone new, you just felt on edge, prickly. Something felt off and you couldn't explain it or exactly put your finger on it, you just knew.

That was your intuition.

Trust it!

Oracle cards are a wonderful way to tap into your intuition if you're looking for a little extra help or support. There are many types available so you're sure to find a set that calls to you.

Or you can practise your intuition with a regular set of playing cards.

Shuffle them and turn one over, place your hand over the card and see if you can feel into which card it is.

You can also go out on a colour walk.

Just take a walk somewhere, and as you walk look out for something red, then orange, then yellow, then green, then blue, then purple and then white.

If you find things easily then you can go through the colours again with the following rule: you're not allowed to choose the same items you found last time.

If you get bored of colours you can spell out your name and find things that begin with each letter of your name.

You may be surprised at the things you find.

Crown Chakra

Crown chakra or Sahasrara: I know.

Situated at the top of the head.

Represented by the colour violet or clear/transparent.

Physical symptoms of imbalance include dizziness, confusion, mental fog, anxiety, stress and other mental health disorders. Skin disorders such as rashes, acne and eczema.

You can help to keep this area balanced with silence or by listening to nature that surrounds you, walking outdoors, sitting under a tree, reading, or even taking a daytime nap.

When this chakra is balanced you feel a strong sense of connection to your spirituality or faith. You are wise and understanding. There is a sense of allowing and accepting without the need to have all the answers in advance or have all the next steps laid out. There is trust in divine timing and that what is meant for you will come to you.

If this area is overactive, you may experience a disconnect and prefer to distance yourself from other people. There may be a struggle to choose or make decisions. It can cause you to have a sense of elitism or superiority over others and for this reason you will lack empathy.

If too little energy flows here then you may lack inspiration, feel greedy, require material objects, and have mental fog, meaning a mind full of jumbled and cloudy thoughts. Nothing seems cohesive or makes any sense.

This chakra is your seat of consciousness and awareness. It brings you knowledge, wisdom, understanding, spiritual connection and bliss. It allows you to see the bigger picture and to live unapologetically in the moment. You will see the beauty in the smallest of things.

A balanced crown chakra brings feelings of serenity, joy and deep peace about life. It allows for differing levels of excitement, feelings of fulfilment, celebration and self-worth.

When you are working on the energy of the crown chakra sometimes an energetic shift, an up – level, can happen instantly. You will get an immediate sense or feeling and know that something has lifted, changed or been released.

Sometimes the change happens more gradually; you may not even be aware of it occurring, as it will take some time to notice it.

Allow your experience to be exactly as it is; don't be tempted to try to rush the results. There is no right or wrong here. You are not in competition with anyone else on the same journey. You are simply allowing a natural progression of events in your own time.

The crown chakra is your place of *I Know*, and I believe that knowledge is power. As you learn more and get to know more, then you can do more, and you can make more deeply informed decisions. More options become available to you simply because you know of their existence.

But, the true power of knowledge lies in its application. When you learn something new, for it to be effective, for it to benefit you in any way, it has to be implemented or actioned.

Taking the time to learn means nothing if you simply store the knowledge away and ignore it.

~

What is the difference between knowledge and wisdom?

The way you acquire knowledge is external, something you actively go and seek for yourself: you study, read, research, take courses or classes, you have encounters or conversations with other people.

When you then turn that knowledge inwardly and apply it, you alchemise it into wisdom.

Knowledge is an external gathering of information imparted by others – it is action and doing.

Wisdom is an internal reflection of how you've witnessed others and yourself implementing this knowledge. It is reflection and being.

Not everything new that you learn will be immediately applicable or relevant to you, and this is when you can store your knowledge away. Not to be forgotten but there for you to re-access it and apply it when the time is right.

You have to look within and trust your intuition to know when this time is.

The path to wisdom is never a straight line; it's a spiral. You continually come back to things you thought you already understood to gain more knowledge to see deeper truths and meanings.

Sometimes when you learn something, when you are given a new piece of information, you think *of course, that's so obvious, how did I not know that already*, but that's why knowledge is so wonderful – it becomes amplified when it is shared for the benefit of others.

When you know more about yourself, who you are, and what you need in order to thrive, then you can do more to help yourself, as you have more choices or options that are available to you.

I'm sure that many times before you have faced a fork in the road and a decision needed to be made. It was through recollection of stored knowledge, recalling memories of similar events that have happened before, that helped you realise you already had the wisdom inside to know how you wanted to move forward.

The more decisions you need to make, the less time you take to ponder all the what-ifs. That need to write out lists is reduced, and there will be less time spent procrastinating over all the choices and their subsequent outcomes, as you will just trust your intuition, your inner compass. You will cal on your inner wisdom, and know what is right for you and your highest good more easily.

You alone are responsible for what you create an abundance of in your life.

Are you attracting more turbulent times or do you allow for ease and flow?

When you live fully in the area of the crown chakra it allows for you to take responsibility for your own life. To take responsibility means that you make yourself accountable for you. Your thoughts, your words, your actions, your choices, your behaviours and your interactions with others.

Responsibility puts you in the position of choice.

You already know that you can't always choose who or what enters or leaves your life. You can't choose what other people think, say or do. But you can decide how you choose to let all of that affect you.

You have the choice to choose acceptance of a situation over wanting to control a situation. You get to pause to take the time to respond rather than react before you do or say anything.

A response is:

- Calmer
- An action chosen by conscious choice
- Mindful of everybody involved
- Suspending judgement in order to see the bigger picture
- Listening to the other side and then choosing how to proceed

A reaction is:

- In the heat of the moment
- Impulsive
- Governed by a sense of urgency and so rushed decisions are made

- Fuelled by emotion
- For self-preservation, fight or flight

When you take responsibility for making these choices it changes your entire energy and puts you in a higher vibration for both body and mind.

Energetically the crown chakra has a connection back to the root chakra, as they are at both ends of the chakra system. Think of the root as being like a recycling centre: it helps you to have a good sift and sort out and get rid of what you no longer need. The crown is like a trophy cabinet: it's where you store all of the high vibration energy that you wish to access daily with ease.

Journal Prompts

Root Chakra Journal Prompts

- What seeds am I setting?
- What do I want to do, be and have?
- What boundaries am I putting into place?
  - (Make a goal surrounding your boundaries. Decide on something you will say yes to more often or something you need to say no to more often, then all of your words, deeds, thoughts, and actions will be about bringing this boundary to life. Write your boundaries down and let the universe know you're putting that energy out there, that this is what you are currently working on.)
- What are my current blocks, fears, or shadows preventing me from naming my boundaries?
- What feelings about myself do I hold here?

- Where do they come from? Is it from family, friends, or are they things that have been said directly to me? Are they just things I believe to be true?
- How does this manifest/appear in my everyday life?
- What else does this space want me to know and begin working on?
- Who am I?
  - (Begin with *I am* and then with no other voice or opinion in your mind but your own, write out exactly who you are.)

Sacral Chakra Journal Prompts

- What beliefs and feelings about creativity do I hold here?
- What is a creative activity I've always wanted to try but never got round to?
- What are my beliefs or feelings about abundance?
- What beliefs or feelings do I have about my connection to others?
- Where do these feelings or beliefs come from, me or an outside influence? (Wherever they are from, if they no longer serve a purpose I can let go of them.)
- How does all of the above manifest day to day for me?
- What can I do on a daily basis that provides me more opportunities for fun?
- What else does this space want me to know?

Solar Plexus Journal Prompts

- Do I live my life in alignment with my true beliefs and the values that I hold?
- What beliefs or feelings about my personal power lie here?
    - (When do I feel most/least confident?)
- Do I have boundaries: do I confidently say no or yes? (Remember, no is a whole sentence, and my power is in knowing my own mind.)
- Do I have a change in mind I wish to make? What is it?
- What beliefs or feelings about self-assurance and self-respect lie here?
- Where do they come from?
- What does the word positivity mean to me?
- How does this confidence or the lack of confidence manifest in my everyday life?
- What else does this space want me to know?

Heart Chakra Journal Prompts

- How do I love myself and those around me?
- Do I set conditions consciously/subconsciously for how I will love or be loved?
- Do I have a free heart that accepts all?
- What are my beliefs about love?
- What are my beliefs and feelings about compassion?
- What are my beliefs and feelings around sorrow?
- Where or why might I be obstructing or preventing love from coming in or out of my life?
- What 5 things do I most love about myself?
- Is there anything else my heart space wants me to know?

Throat Chakra Journal Prompts

- Am I able to communicate freely, authentically and truthfully?
- What are my beliefs or feelings about my power to express myself?
- Is there something I wish I could say but can't? Why can't I?
- What would I say and who would I say it to?
- Do I keep my word? Is this important to me?
- Do I feel my voice is heard when I speak?
- Do I take the time to really listen to others?
- What else does this space want me to know?

Brow Chakra Journal Prompts

- How well do I trust my intuition?
- What beliefs or feelings do I have around my intuition?
- What are my beliefs and feelings surrounding my ability to think and reason?
- How open is my sixth sense?
- Are my decisions guided more by logic or intuition?
- Do I consider myself to be imaginative?
- Where in life am I open - or closed-minded?
- What else does this space want me to know?

Crown Chakra Journal Prompts.

- Do I feel connected to a higher power?
- Am I prepared to take a leap of faith?
- Do I know myself as my highest self?
- What beliefs about connection to Source, Spirit, God/Goddess do I hold?
- Draw how open I feel my crown is in terms of an open flower.
- What feelings or beliefs do I hold about my spiritual expression?
- Where did these feelings or beliefs come from?
- Do I understand my soul's purpose: do I know what I came here to do?
- What else does this space want me to know?

Affirmations to Support the Chakras

Affirmations for Root.

I feel deeply rooted.

I am connected to my body.

I feel safe and secure.

Just like a tree or a star I have a right to be here.

I stand for my values and truth.

I have what I need.

I nurture my body with healthy food, clean water, exercise, relaxation, and connection with nature.

I am open to all possibilities.

I am grateful for all the challenges that have helped me grow and transform.

I know my own beliefs, I set my own boundaries.

Affirmations for Sacral

I love and enjoy my body.

I have healthy boundaries.

I am passionate.

I deserve to be loved.

I feel pleasure and abundance with every breath I take.

I know how to take care of my needs.

I value and respect my body.

Emotions are the language of my soul.

I am at peace.

I am alive, connected and aware.

Affirmations for Solar Plexus

I love and accept myself.

I am worthy of love, kindness and respect.

I am strong, courageous and stand up for myself.

I always choose the best for myself.

I express myself in a powerful way.

I am proud of my achievements.

I direct my own life.

I appreciate my strengths.

I am free to choose in any situation.

I seek opportunities for growth.

Affirmations for Heart

I am open to love.

I deeply and completely love and accept all versions of me.

I nurture my inner child.

I am wanted and loved.

I forgive myself.

I am grateful for all the challenges that helped me transform into who I am today.

I am connected to other human beings.

I accept things as they are.

I can let go of the past.

I live in balance, in a state of gratitude.

Affirmations for Throat

I am open, clear, and honest in my communication.

I communicate my feelings with ease.

I have the right to speak my truth.

I express myself creatively through speech, song, writing or art.

I have a strong will that lets me resolve my challenges.

I have integrity.

It is my pleasure to share my experiences, wisdom, and knowledge.

I express my gratitude for the life I lead.

I know when it is my time to listen.

I express love and kindness every time I speak.

Affirmations for Brow

My life moves effortlessly.

I am in touch with my inner guidance.

I listen to my deepest wisdom.

I seek to learn from my life experiences.

I am wise and intuitive.

I forgive the past.

I am open to inspiration and bliss.

I am the source of my truth.

I listen to the wisdom of others.

I know that all is well in my world.

Affirmations for Crown

I am part of the divine.

I honour the divine within me.

I cherish my spirit.

I seek experiences that nourish me.

I am open to letting go of past attachments.

I live in the present moment.

I am grateful for all the goodness in my life.

I love and accept myself.

My life moves with grace.

I am at peace.

I have unlimited potential.

Gemstones & Crystals to Support the Chakras

There are many ways to work with crystals.

You can simply place them around your home, on window ledges, on your desk or your bedside table. You can put them in a small pouch and carry them in your handbag. You can wear them directly as jewellery, or you can meditate whilst holding them.

Holding a stone whilst you meditate is wonderful, as the feeling of touch overrides your desire to think. You are more receptive to the meditation you are listening to as holding the stone and perhaps turning it over in your hand, quietens your mind.

Complement or Clash?

I'm often asked about which crystals work well together and I hope this goes some way towards providing an answer.

If you are new to crystals, I would advise using them one at a time to begin with.

Going from having none to suddenly having crystals dotted everywhere can result in an energy overload which will result in the opposite of your desired effect.

You may end up feeling sluggish with a headache if you invite in too much too soon.

Whilst there isn't a wrong way to use crystals, being mindful of the colour wheel is a great way to access your stone's most complementary energy.

Firstly, there are the black, brown, silver, and grey colours. These all are grounding stones that help you to feel safe and secure and that your most basic of needs are met.

Then there are warm colours.

Reds, oranges and yellows. Warm colours are energising, encouraging. They aid in the development of passion, creativity and abundance, bravery, luck, success, and self-confidence. These are the get– moving, motivating, increasing stones.

Then there are cool colours.

Blues, indigo, violet and white. Cool colours are receptive energy; they soothe and aid love, calm, peace, knowledge, sleep, physical, mental and spiritual growth. These are the slowing down, calming, decreasing, inward-looking stones.

Green and pink lie in the middle and are for balance.

If you were, for example, to choose a carnelian and sodalite – one is orange and the other blue – nothing much would happen, as the carnelian has a high-frequency vibration and the sodalite a low, so the 2 energies just cancel each other out.

Stones of the same colour or that lie next to each other on a colour wheel are usually compatible on an energetic level and a wonderful way to pair or group your stones.

~

Gemstones and crystals that are associated with the **root chakra** are typically black, brown, or red. Useful stones include:

- Brown jasper
- Red jasper
- Smoky quartz
- Hematite
- Garnet
- Bloodstone
- Onyx
- Ruby
- Fire opal

Gemstones and crystals that are associated with the **sacral chakra** are typically brown or orange. Useful stones include:

- Carnelian
- Fire opal
- Sunstone
- Orange calcite
- Tigers eye
- Orange jasper

Gemstones and crystals that are associated with the **solar plexus chakra** are typically light orange or yellow. Useful stones include:

- Amber
- Citrine
- Yellow sapphire
- Moonstone
- Yellow jasper

Gemstones and crystals that are associated with the **heart chakra** are typically light pink or green. Useful stones include:

- Rose quartz
- Pink sapphire
- Ruby
- Green aventurine
- Emerald
- Green tourmaline
- Peridot
- Jade
- Green moss agate

Gemstones and crystals that are associated with the **throat chakra** are typically blue. Useful stones include:

- Lapis lazuli
- Aquamarine
- Sapphire
- Blue topaz

- Sodalite
- Blue lace agate
- Blue apatite
- Turquoise

Gemstones and crystals that are associated with the **brow chakra** are typically purple. Useful stones include:

- Amethyst
- Angelite
- Celestite
- Iolite
- Fluorite

Gemstones and crystals that are associated with the **crown chakra** are clear or milky. Useful stones include:

- Clear quartz
- Diamond
- Zirconia

- Opalite
- Selenite

If you are more used to crystals and have already experienced working with them individually, then learning how to pair them up is a wonderful way to amplify an intent or desire.

Crystals pairings for:

Love: in general, or for family and friends

Rose quartz and green aventurine.

Romantic love and relationships

Amethyst and rose quartz.

New job or interview

Green aventurine and citrine.

Creativity/motivation/energy/the ability to get things done

Citrine and carnelian.

Sleep

Amethyst and rose quartz.

Focus/determination/concentration

Fluorite and amethyst.

Grounding

Red jasper and carnelian.

Manifesting

Citrine and rose quartz.

Meditation

Whichever colour or stone you feel most drawn to.

Hormonal imbalances

Different coloured moonstones.

Fear, worry, and bad dreams

Smoky quartz and black tourmaline.

Stress and anxiety

Rose quartz for inner peace.

Amethyst to calm.

Sodalite for the throat chakra to communicate your troubles or the need for help.

Green aventurine for the release of old patterns and habits.

Easing a cold

Moss agate to balance your immune system.

Sodalite for sore throats.

Carnelian for vitality.

Connection

Honesty

Alignment

Knowledge

Responsibility

Alchemy

Thanks for Reading!

I know that there are many books on this subject out there, but you chose this book, and for that, I am truly grateful.

I hope that this has explained the basics of chakra work and energy alchemy, in a way that has you excited and motivated to begin to implement it.

Energy Alchemy is not just a process it's a whole way of living.

A lifestyle that helps you to transmute the energy of mind, body and spirit.

To begin with you may find it easier to implement your new found knowledge by working from root through to crown. But as you become more familiar with the content of this book and your own inner energy, you will find that you can jump in and out of the different chapters, to support where you are currently at.

Thank you for being the Curious Creatrix that you are, for allowing me into your world for a little while and for making space for me in your energy, as I hold space for you.

If you enjoyed this book then please do recommend it to a friend or leave me a review.

If you would like to continue being in my world then we can alchemise a whole heap more energy together.

You can find me in my Facebook group, Room to Breathe – Crystal Connections.

Or on my website www.aroomtobreathe.co.uk

Thank you again Curious Creatrix. Now go and alchemise your energy to unapologetically create a life you love.

A life full of intention for all that you came here to do, be and have

As ever, with the warmest of wishes and sincerest gratitude,

Lynsey xxx

Printed in Great Britain
by Amazon